This Orchard
book belongs to

_____

_____

_____

D0184148

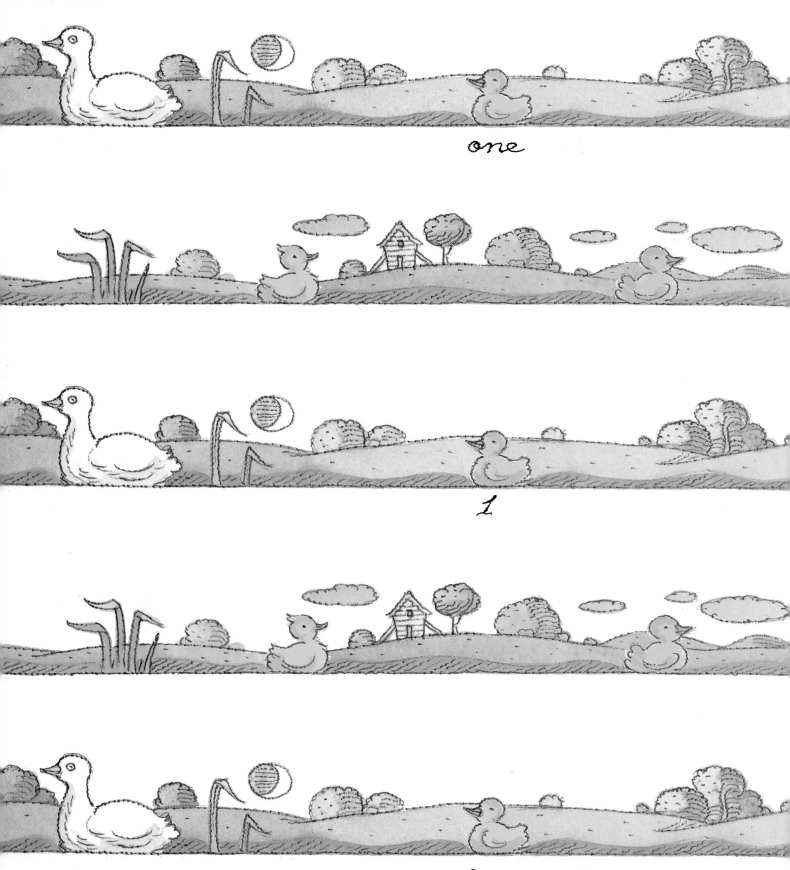

one

1

one

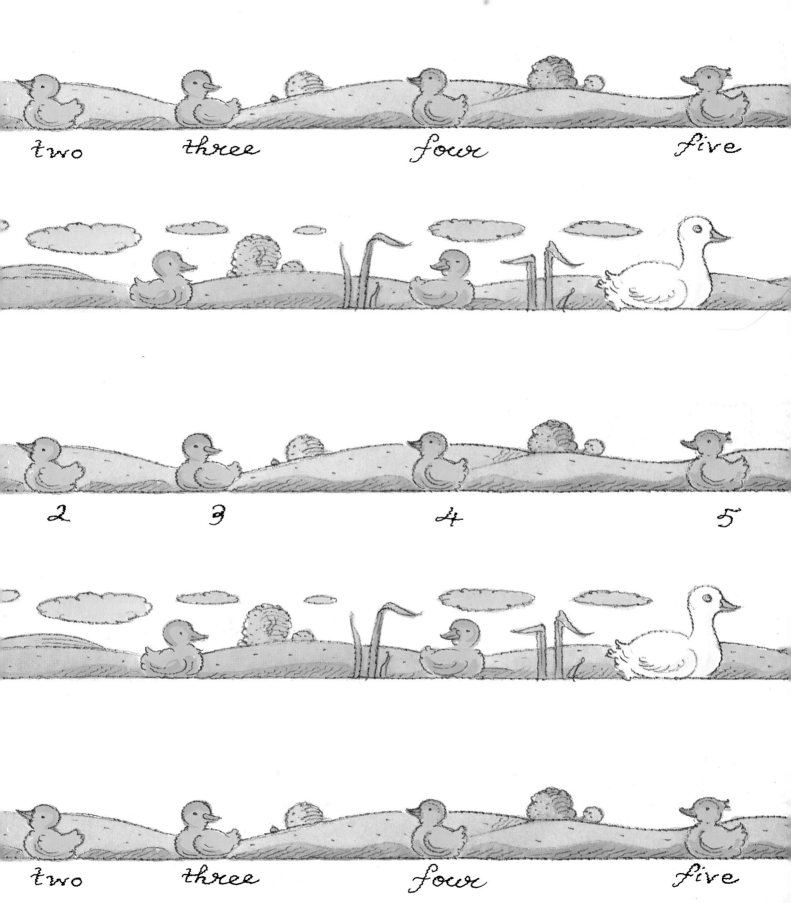

two   three   four   five

2   3   4   5

two   three   four   five

For Emma

ORCHARD BOOKS

338 Euston Road, London NW1 3BH

Orchard Books Australia

Level 17/207 Kent Street, Sydney, NSW 2000

First published in 1992 by Orchard Books
First published in paperback in 1993
This edition published in 2007

ISBN 978 1 84616 579 5

1 3 5 7 9 10 8 6 4 2

Printed in China

Orchard Books is a division of Hachette Children's Books

Five Little DUCKS

IAN BECK

ORCHARD BOOKS

Five little ducks went swimming one day,
Over the hills and far away.

Mother duck said, "Quack, quack, quack, quack."
But only four little ducks came back.

Four little ducks went swimming one day,
Over the hills and far away.

Mother duck said, "Quack, quack, quack, quack."
But only three little ducks came back.

Three little ducks went swimming one day,
Over the hills and far away.

Mother duck said, "Quack, quack, quack, quack."
But only two little ducks came back.

Two little ducks went swimming one day,

Over the hills and far away.

Mother duck said, "Quack, quack, quack, quack."
But only one little duck came back.

One little duck went swimming one day,

Over the hills

and far away.

Mother duck said, "Quack, quack, quack, quack."

And all her five little ducks came back.

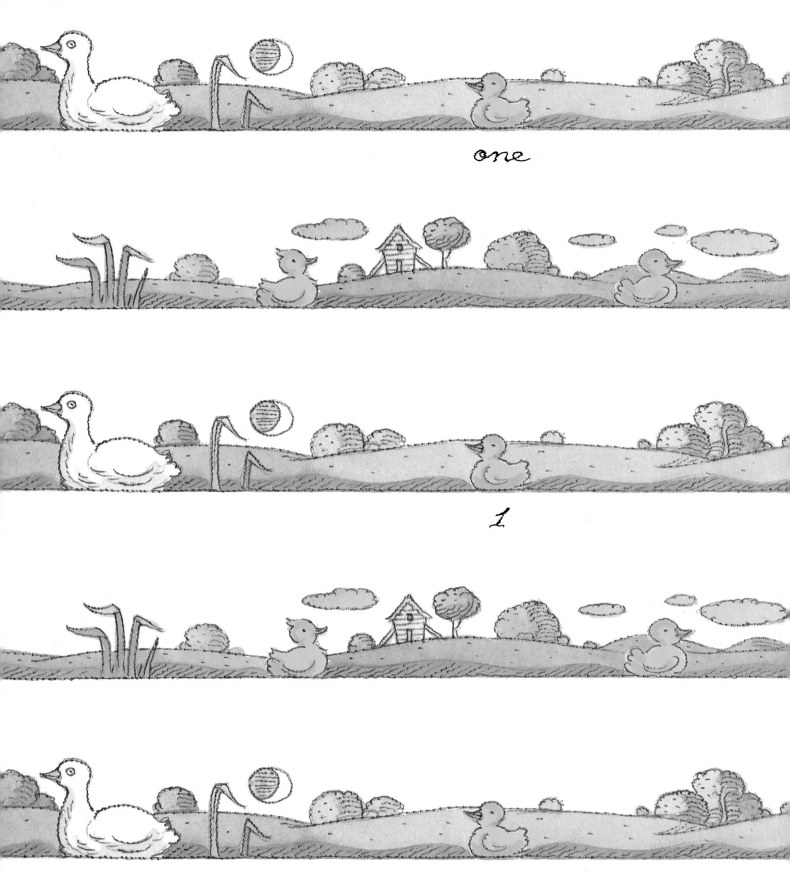

one

1

one

two   *three*   *four*   *five*

2   3   4   5

two   *three*   *four*   *five*